O'Diddy

By Jocelyn Stevenson
Illustrated by Sue Truesdell

A STEPPING STONE BOOK
Random House 🏠 New York

To Freddie, Ela, Tom,
and their imaginary friends

Text copyright © 1988 by Jocelyn Stevenson. Illustrations copyright © 1988 by Sue Truesdell.
All rights reserved under International and Pan-American Copyright Conventions.
Published in the United States by Random House, Inc., New York, and simultaneously in
Canada by Random House of Canada Limited, Toronto.

Library of Congress Cataloging-in-Publication Data:
Stevenson, Jocelyn. O'Diddy / by Jocelyn Stevenson ; illustrated by Sue Truesdell.
p. cm.—(A Stepping stone book) SUMMARY: Nine-year-old Boon has grown too old to see
her imaginary friend O'Diddy, so in his lonesome desperation he concocts a scheme to force
her into remembering him. ISBN: 0-394-89609-2 (pbk.); 0-394-99609-7 (lib. bdg.)
[1. Imaginary playmates—Fiction.] I. Truesdell, Sue, ill. II. Title. PZ7.S84760d 1988
[E]—dc19 87-22676

Manufactured in the United States of America 1 2 3 4 5 6 7 8 9 0

Contents

1. Me

My name is O'Diddy, and I'm an imaginary
friend.

Right away I can hear you thinking, What?
Is this guy a lunatic? Imaginary friends don't
write books. Imaginary friends are what little kids make up when they want someone to
play with. Really, I'm taking this book back
to the store and asking for a refund.

Not so fast. Aren't you going to give me a
chance? It's not easy for an imaginary friend
to write a book, you know. The least you can
do is read it. Let's make a deal. Four is my
lucky number. If you get to chapter 4 and
you're still worried about whether I'm telling
the truth, then you can take the book back to

the store. Or better yet, give it to a friend—a real friend.

Now that we've got that out of the way, I'll keep going. I'm sure you are incredibly smart, but I bet you don't know a whole lot about imaginary friends.

"What's there to know?" you say.

Well, I say, "Plenty!"

I bet you think you humans make us up and we're there while you believe in us and the minute you stop believing, we're gone. Admit it. That's what you think, isn't it?

Well, you're wrong.

This is how it goes. One day your imaginary friend suddenly appears. You play for a while and before long, you realize you've never had a friend like this before—always on your side, always there when you need him. Or her. Or it. Well, everything is fantastic until one day—*boom!* You go to school. Then what happens? You make all sorts of real friends and you forget about your imaginary friend. If anyone asks you about him, you say, "Don't be silly. There's no such thing."

If that's what you think, then what about me? This book isn't writing itself, you know.

The truth is, there are such things as imaginary friends. And believe it or not—which you probably don't—they do not disappear. Your imaginary friend is still there. You just can't see or hear him anymore. Or let me say that another way. It's not that you can't see or hear him . . . it's that you won't.

I ask you—how do you think it feels to be invisible? I tell you—it's the pits. And that's why I'm writing this book. If I can save just one imaginary friend a tiny bit of the pain I've suffered, then this whole book will be worth it.

2. Boon

I guess the first thing I ought to do is tell you about the person who's driven me to expose my deepest feelings to a complete stranger. (Just think. If you read this whole book, you'll know almost everything about me and what will I know about you? Nothing. That just goes to show how desperate I am.) Her name is Beatrice Odile Olivia Noodleman, Boon for short. As I write this she's eight and a half—far too old to have an imaginary friend, or so she would think if she thought about it. Which she doesn't.

Anyway, when Boon was about three years old, she wanted a friend more than anything in the world. Hard to believe, looking at her now. She's got lots of friends, and she's absolutely crazy about those Bandello twins. But wait. I'm getting ahead of myself. All that comes later.

Back to Boon. When she was a lonely little three-year-old with no friends and busy parents, she wished for a friend. Naturally, the Dispatcher got wind of it.

If you don't mind, I'm going to use a page or two here to give you some background information. The Dispatcher is very important. She's what you might call the boss of us imaginary friends. She knows which kids need imaginary friends when, and figures out which imaginary friend would best handle the job. Then she tells that imaginary friend to get out there and do it. She dispatches us. That's why she's called the Dispatcher.

Well, one day I was sitting in the Dispatchery—that's the place where we imaginary friends hang out, waiting to be dispatched—with my friend and colleague Barloff the bear. The Dispatcher had just given Barloff an under-the-bed job, and he was really looking forward to it.

"Can you believe it, O'Diddy?" he growled.

"I just have to lie there! My human won't sleep unless I'm under the bed to keep away the witches. What witches? There are no witches! It's the perfect job!"

Suddenly the Dispatcher appeared. "O'Diddy?" she said. "Follow me!" And she headed for her office.

I looked at Barloff and gulped. What had I

done this time? The last time the Dispatcher had said "O'Diddy, follow me," she'd yelled at me for filling the gnome's hat with dirt. How she found out, I'll never know, but let me tell you something—that gnome deserved it. He was a real pain. Still is. But more on that later.

When I walked into her office, the Dispatcher was hunting around in her file cabinet. She's not very big, and to tell the truth, she looks more like a barn owl than a person. But in the world of imaginary friends, we don't pay much attention to what someone looks like. What matters is how he or she *feels*. And I don't mean sticky or prickly or squishy. Remember, we imaginary friends don't have real skin the way you do. We have to go by what a person feels like to be with. And the Dispatcher feels like the sky and a shopping center—wise and busy at the same time.

"O'Diddy," she said, pulling out my file. "I've got a job for you."

"A job?" I almost croaked. Here I thought she was going to yell at me and instead she was giving me a job! But before you get too caught up in the excitement, I have to tell you this was not the first time those exact words had gone from her mouth into my ears. I confess. I had not exactly been the most successful imaginary friend. I mean, my first time out I was dispatched to a little girl who really, really liked my idea about making a double chocolate fudge swirl cake in the bathtub. She liked it so much that she tried to do it. That was the end of that job. When the Dispatcher redispatched me, I got a great little kid named Mortimer who let me decorate the living room. It was fantastic! Pink crayon clouds carefully outlined with yellow tempera paint all over the room. Very tasteful. Only, Mort's mother didn't think so.

To hand it to Mort, he did give credit where credit was due. He pointed at me and said, "But *he* did it!"

His mother just glowered at him. She couldn't see me, of course. Grownups never can.

"Oh, did he?" she said, or rather, hollered. And that's how I got my name.

"So, O'Diddy," said the Dispatcher, staring at my file. Then she pulled out a large purple handkerchief and blew her nose. It's a great sound when the Dispatcher blows her nose—like when you've almost finished the glue and you're squeezing the last drop out of the bottle—enough to crack you up.

"And what, may I ask, is so funny?" The Dispatcher stared deep into my eyes as if she could see my brain. I started to feel all hot inside.

"Nothing," I lied. How do you tell someone that the sound of her blowing her nose is the funniest thing you've ever heard in your life? You can't. "I'm—I'm just happy about getting a job!"

"As well you should be," said the Dispatcher, once again looking through my file. "According to my records, this will be your third assignment."

"That's right," I said. "Third time lucky!"

"Let's hope so," said the Dispatcher sternly. Then she closed the file and looked at me. "O'Diddy, do you know what happens if you lose this job?"

I nodded and looked at the floor. "I'm out."

The thought was so horrible I could barely say it.

"I'm afraid that's how it is," the Dispatcher said.

"But I'm going to make this one work, I promise!" I said, and I meant it, too. "I won't make cakes in the bathtub and I won't paint the walls. I'll be good, you'll see! And I'll stay with this human forever and ever and ever and ever and ever—"

"I get the message, O'Diddy," interrupted the Dispatcher. I guess I'd kind of gotten carried away. "But as you know, being a good imaginary friend isn't easy. Particularly when your human stops seeing you."

"Oh, don't worry, Dispatcher. That won't happen to me!" I said confidently. If only I knew then what I know now. I would've kept my mouth shut.

The Dispatcher just shook her head. "It's a rare and special human who keeps the connection," she sighed. For one moment she felt deep and dark, like the sky at night. "Anyway," she said, quickly getting back to business, "report to 245 Oak Street. You'll find your human playing in the garden."

Then the Dispatcher reached for her handkerchief. She was just about to blow her nose again when she caught my eye. "If you thought the last time was funny, listen to this." She took a big breath and blew. I couldn't help it. I laughed my head off. And you know what? She laughed too! And she felt like the sun on a cloudless day.

To make a long story less long, Boon and I hit it off from the moment we met. Two of a kind. She had brown hair; I had brown hair. She wore glasses; I wore glasses. She was sort of skinny, and so was I. When I first saw her, she was making leaf and pebble soup. My favorite.

"Hello," I said.

"Hello," she said. "Want some soup?"

"Love some," I said. She handed me a cup.

"It needs ketchup," she said, and dumped a handful of mud into my soup. Not only was she nice, but she could cook!

"What's your name?" she asked.

"O'Diddy," I answered. "Your name's Boon, right?"

"Yup," she said. Then she cocked her head

and looked at me. "You know something? You feel like a birthday party."

"And you feel like a summer day."

As I said, Boon and I hit it off from the moment we met.

And to make matters better, the grownups in her house never seemed to mind what we did. No kidding. I mean, you'd think Mrs. Noodleman would've had a fit when we used her best hat for a magic show and the crack-an-egg-in-a-hat-say-abracadabra-and-pull-out-a-whole-egg trick accidentally didn't work. But all she said was that egg is very good for your hair, and besides, she'd stopped wearing hats to work anyway. That's some kind of mother!

For nearly three years Boon and I did everything together. And we liked all the same things—card games, old cartoons, chewy cookies, strawberry ice cream, orange socks, and stories with wolves in them. It was fantastic. Okay, so in the very back of my mind, where you put things like your shoe size and the color of your toothbrush, I was worried that one day Boon wouldn't see me anymore. It had happened to all of my friends.

But they didn't have humans like Boon. She was rare and special. She would never stop seeing me. Ever. That's what I kept telling myself, but I wore a green and orange striped shirt with fluorescent socks and a bow tie to match just to make sure.

3. Out of Sight, Out of Mind

Guess what. The socks didn't help. Neither did the bow tie.

"O'Diddy," Boon said one day in the middle of a game of lions. "I've got to go to school."

"Why?" I said.

"Mom says."

"Oh." I crawled into the lion's den, which was under the bed.

"O'Diddy?" Boon crawled in after me. "I'm scared."

"What's there to be scared of?" I asked. "There aren't any wolves at school, are there?"

"No, but I don't know any of the children except for Alistair." Alistair lived next door and once put a worm down Boon's shirt. We didn't like Alistair. "And"—her voice was trembling now—"I don't know the . . . the teacher or . . . or . . . anything!"

"Well, you know me, don't you?" I put my arm around her and gave her a big hug. "I'll always be with you."

"I know, but . . . " Boon didn't finish the sentence. Boon was a worrier—still is—and no matter what I said, she'd worry anyway.

Well, when we got to school, we sat in the corner just to check the place out. Suddenly a girl with long blond hair ran over and tried to sit on top of me! It was Cassie Bandello.

"Hey! Watch out!" said Boon. "You're sitting on O'Diddy!"

Cassie leaped up and stared at the chair. Naturally she didn't see anything.

"Hey, Frank!" she called to her twin brother. "This girl said I sat on her diddy!"

"She didn't say 'on her diddy,' you numbskull!" I shouted. "She said 'on O'Diddy'! That's me!"

"I didn't say 'on my diddy,' " repeated Boon. "I said 'on O'Diddy.' He's my friend."

I thought that would do it. I thought Cassie

would say "Oh, sorry. I hope I didn't squash him." But instead, the worst possible thing happened. The Bandello twins started to laugh. They didn't know what Boon was talking about. Unfortunately, when some people don't know what you're talking about, they laugh. It's stupid, I know, but what are you going to do about it? Anyway, when they started to laugh, so did everybody else—even the ones who had their own imaginary friends standing there right next to them! The nerve!

One of the imaginary friends—in fact, it was the gnome I mentioned earlier—leaned over and whispered, "It's happening to you, pal. Your human is going to stop seeing you! Take it from me, it's no fun. I've been invisible since yesterday. Watch!" And he danced up and down in front of his human, waggling his pointy little ears and shouting "Waheemaaah! Waheemaaah!" Sure enough, his human didn't even blink an eye.

"Tragic, isn't it?" he grunted.

"Well, it won't happen to me!" I told him. What did he know anyway? "Boon's not like your human. She's rare and special, aren't you, Boon?"

But Boon wasn't listening. She was staring wide-eyed at the beautiful Cassie Bandello.

"What did you say I sat on again?" Cassie giggled.

Boon turned to me. She looked okay on the outside, but I could tell she was messed up on the inside.

"Go on, Boon," I said. "Tell 'em I'm here. Just because those dopes can't see me doesn't mean—"

"Nothing," said Boon, not even having the courtesy to let me finish my sentence. "I was just joking."

And from that moment on, Boon stopped seeing or hearing me.

"Told you so! Told you so! Oh, I love saying that!" yelled the gnome, jumping up and down. He poked me in the ribs. "Now they see you, now they don't!"

"Oh, be quiet!" I felt like pulling off his stupid little green cap and stamping on it. "Boon's different! Different, I tell you!" But though I could shout "Boon's different!" until Christmas, the fact of the matter was, she wasn't. I was invisible and that was that.

• • •

Don't get me wrong—being invisible does have its advantages. It means I can do whatever I want and Boon would never think to blame me. Like the other day, when I hid one of her sneakers. Boon thought she'd lost it. And when she finally got up the nerve to tell her father, he was not happy.

"Who's got time to buy you another pair?" he said. "Not me! You're old enough to keep track of your own clothes. You'll just have to hop to gym class. Have you looked under your bed?"

Of course Boon had looked under her bed. But I hadn't hidden her sneaker there, had I? Too obvious. I'd put it in the closet behind the big bad wolf puppet we used to play with. I thought she'd get the hint. I thought she'd find it and say "Hmmmm. I know I didn't put this sneaker in here. Hmmmm. This is the puppet O'Diddy always liked so much. Hmmmmmm. Maybe *he* hid my sneaker! Yeah! That's what happened! O'Diddy, where are you?" But no. She never even thought to look in there.

So her sneaker's still there, and she's having to save up her allowance to buy a new pair. In the meantime, she's taking gym class in her bedroom slippers. It's okay for gymnastics, but have you ever tried playing kickball in slippers? Ouch!

Now I wish I'd never hidden that stupid sneaker in the first place. This is where being invisible has its disadvantages. You see, imaginary friends cannot help their humans unless their humans ask them to. That's the rule. Of course, we can do whatever we want to try to make them ask us (like hide sneakers). But we can't actually help them unless they ask.

When you're visible, this isn't a problem. Your human steps in something disgusting with her new party shoes. She sees you doubled over with laughter and says, "O'Diddy, quit laughing and help me find something to wipe this yuck off with!" So you stop laughing and point out a big leaf she can use. She asked, you helped.

But when you're invisible it's a different story. Unless she says "O'Diddy, please help me find my sneaker," there's no way I can help her find it.

I'd like to be able to say "Okay, so Boon

doesn't want to see me. Okay, so she's not rare and special. Well, that's her problem" and leave it at that. But I can't. And believe me, I'm getting really sick of hiding sneakers and making faucets drip and messing up drawers to let Boon know I'm around. But I'm getting even sicker of her not understanding. Instead of saying "O'Diddy, cut it out. I know it's you," what does she say? She says "Isn't that strange?" and "What a coincidence!"

Coincidence nothing—it's me! Open your eyes, girl! It wasn't a coincidence that every bit of toast you made the other day burned no matter how much you twiddled the little dial on the toaster! It wasn't a coincidence that one of your favorite orange socks went missing! It wasn't a coincidence that your entire shell collection ended up under your pillow! It was me, trying to get through to you! If you haven't got the brains to put two and two together, then maybe you're not worth the trouble! That's right! Maybe I should just relax and enjoy being invisible! But I can't! And you know why? No, not because you're my third assignment! Not because I have

nowhere else to go! BUT BECAUSE I LOVE YOU!
THAT'S WHY!!

Wait a minute. Wait a minute. What am I doing? You're not Boon. Listen, I'm sorry. I guess I just got carried away. But now you can see what you humans do to us imaginary types. You make us nuts! I'm fed up, I tell you! I've had it!

And that's why I started to make a plan.

4. My Plan

Before I tell you about my plan, I want to say that I hope you're still reading this. I gave you until chapter 4 to decide whether or not you wanted to keep the book, remember? Well, here we are at chapter 4. So what's it going to be? Keep the book or give it away? If you decide to keep it, thank you very much and please keep on reading. You're the kind of friend an imaginary friend needs. If you decide to give it away, good-bye and no hard feelings. You may close the book . . . now!

If you can't decide what to do, give it another chapter. Please? I promise I won't yell anymore.

Now, back to my plan.

Remember the Bandello twins, Cassie and Frank? The ones who laughed? Well, they are now the most popular kids in the school. Don't ask me why.

No, no, no—I take that back. It's not the Bandellos' fault Boon can't see me anymore. They really deserve to be popular. From what I've seen of them, they're nice and fun and smart, and Frank does a great walrus imitation. And the clincher is that their dad has a really bizarro job. He makes props for movies—movies called *The Slimebug* and *Planet of the Giant Lice*. Pretty amazing, huh? Anyway, the Bandellos live in the big old house on South Avenue. People say they got the house for a song because it's haunted. If you ask me, it's not haunted. If you ask me, whoever lived in the house before the Bandellos had an imaginary friend who was trying to get through. If you ask me, what sounded like a ghost going "Woooooooooo!" was just that poor imaginary friend saying "I'm here, you idiot! Right in front of yooooooooou!"

But you didn't ask me, did you?

Right. Since the day Boon decided not to

see or hear me anymore, she's been going to school and to dancing lessons and to recorder lessons and to Brownies, and having all sorts of fun. (But not nearly as much as she'd have with me. Sorry—I just had to say that.) And I've been tagging along, invisible, but loyal to the core. Now and then I try to let her know that I'm around but she's decided I'm not, so that's that. Hence, my plan.

My plan was to get Boon into such a horrible mess that she'd *have* to ask me for help. I know that sounds really mean. But as I said before, I'm desperate.

So what kind of mess could I get Boon into? I could jam her lunch box closed so she couldn't eat. But she'd just ask the janitor if he'd please pry it open, and he would, no problem. So that's out. I could hide her arithmetic book the day before the big test, but then she'd just borrow somebody else's. I could push her into Smelly Smetana so she'd get his cooties, but she always refuses to pretend people have cooties because it's not nice. Deep down inside, I know the words "O'Diddy, please help me get rid of Smelly's cooties" would never pass her lips. So what could I do?

There was only one answer: Wait.

While I waited, things got worse, if that's possible. One night at dinner, Boon's little brother—hold it. I haven't told you about him yet, have I? He arrived when Boon was six, not long after the dreadful day when I became invisible. His name is Philip Isaac Newton Noodleman, or Phinny for short. Anyway, as I was saying, one night at dinner, Phinny insisted that his dad set another place at the table. And you know who it was for? His imaginary friend. And you know who that turned out to be? The gnome! Remember him? He'd given up on his first human and asked to be redispatched. Gnomes have no staying power and absolutely hate being invisible.

"Fancy meeting you here," he said.

"What do you mean?" I said. "I've always been here."

"Where? Under the table?"

He had a point. While he was sitting at the

table because Phinny could see him and give him a chair, I was sitting under it—invisible and forgotten.

Then Boon's mom said, "Boon—remember when you had an imaginary friend? What was his name? O'Malley? No, it was . . . oh, what was it?"

When Boon didn't answer, I pinched the gnome. "Tell them my name!" I demanded. "Now! Before I eat your shoe!"

He leaned over and whispered in Phinny's ear.

"O'Diddy!" said Phinny, clear as a bell.

"O'Diddy! That was it!" said Boon's dad. Then there was a pause. "Phinny, how'd you know that?"

"Gnomey told me," said Phinny cheerfully, and went back to his mashed potatoes.

"Your friend's name was O'Diddy, wasn't it, Boon?" said Boon's mother.

"Come on, Boon!" I yelled. "Tell them about me and all the fun we had!"

"Did I have an imaginary friend?" said Boon. "I don't remember."

When the gnome stuck his silly grinning face under the table to see what I thought of

that, I almost pulled his beard. Something had to be done, and something had to be done fast.

The next day, when Boon and I went to school, I used every possible chance I had to get through to her. I tripped her. I tickled her ear. I made her drop her books. I even turned off the water fountain while she was still drinking. But nothing worked. She didn't have a clue. She just thought it was one of those weird days people have now and then.

Then opportunity came like a bolt of lightning out of a clear blue sky.

When Boon and I were getting ready to go home, Cassie Bandello ran up to Boon. "Hey, Boon! I'm having a slumber party at my house tomorrow night. Me and Ella and Pickle. Do you want to sleep over?"

Now, you have to try to understand how much a simple question like "Do you want to sleep over?" meant to Boon when it came from Cassie Bandello. Though she and Cassie sometimes sat next to each other at lunch, Cassie had never ever invited Boon to her house. And being invited to the big old house on South Avenue was one of the most exciting things that could happen to a third grader.

So when Cassie asked Boon to sleep over—not just to come for lunch or to play in the afternoon, but to come and be with her at her house *all night*—Boon almost died. For a long moment she couldn't make her mouth work. Then Cassie said, "Well? Do you want to sleep over or not?"

"Sure! Yes! Of course!" said Boon, trying to sound cool. "I'll ask my mother."

"You do that," said Cassie. And then she saw Frank. "Hey, jerkhead! Wait for me! Bye, Boon! See you tomorrow!" And she was gone.

"Yeah! See you tomorrow!" said Boon. She just stood there as if her feet were glued to the linoleum and watched the twins go out the door. Then she whispered in a voice so quiet that only I heard, "Oh boy!"

5. On Your Mark

When Boon got home and asked her mother, Mrs. Noodleman said she couldn't say yes until she'd phoned Mrs. Bandello. While Boon stood there ready to burst, Mrs. Noodleman made the call.

"Hello, Francine? This is Chloe Noodleman . . . yes! How are you? I know . . . absolutely ages . . . yes, yes I know . . . isn't it horrible. Rain, rain, rain. It's enough to make you wish you were a duck!"

It went on like this for what seemed like centuries. Whenever Boon tried to get her mother's attention by whispering "Mom! What about the slumber party?" her mother just frowned and waved her away.

"Mmmmmhmmmm . . . Mmmmmhmmmm . . . Mmmmmhmmmm . . . " she said into the telephone. I thought she'd keep saying "Mmmmmhmmmm" until next week. And by then the slumber party would be over.

Finally she said, "Yes . . . awful . . . listen, Francine, the reason I'm calling is Cassie asked Boon to stay overnight . . . right . . . well, I just wanted to check with you first . . . . Three! You *are* a brave woman! . . . Oh, you bet. She's dying to come."

"I am not dying," objected Boon. "Mother! You make me sound like a dork!"

Mrs. Noodleman ignored her. "Okay, we'll drop her off around six. Listen, you and Barney really must come over for dinner sometime. . . . Good . . . I'll call you next week. Bye!"

So it was official. Boon was going to her first slumber party. But this wasn't just any slumber party. This was a slumber party at the Bandellos'!

Little did Boon know that I was going to go too. And even littler did she know that by the end of that slumber party O'Diddy's invisible days would be over.

At least, that's what I planned.

Right after Boon's mom got off the phone, Phinny and the gnome burst into the kitchen. "Hey, Boony!" chirped Phinny. "Look what I got!" But Boon was so happy, she didn't even care that Phinny was wearing her very best necklace—the one with the pink plastic pigs.

"You told him to put that on, didn't you?" I asked the gnome.

He didn't answer. He just smiled his ridiculous gnome smile.

"Well, ha, ha, it didn't make Boon mad," I said. I just wished he'd go away and take Phinny with him. "She's got other things on her mind."

"Like what?" said the gnome.

"Like her first slumber party," I answered. "At the Bandellos'."

"You mean the haunted house on South Avenue? Better you than me, pal. Too bad you can't do anything to help her, 'cause she's going to need it."

"She's going to need help all right," I said to myself. "But not because of any ghosts!"

6. Get Set

The minute Cassie Bandello asked Boon to her house, I knew the time had come for my plan. And you know why? Because Boon would never ever ever ever ever want anything to go wrong in front of Cassie and Frank Bandello. She liked them too much. She wore her hair pulled back like Cassie's, rolled up one sleeve of her blouse the way Cassie did, and even turned down the top two inches of her knee socks, just like Cassie. Boon didn't know Frank very well. But if I've got my facts straight, and I do, Frank Bandello, with his curly hair and big eyes, gets more valentines than anybody else in his class. Even in July.

So the Bandellos' house was the last place

Boon would want to find herself in a mess. That's why it was such a perfect time for my plan.

And my plan was to lock her in the bathroom.

I should really say, my plan *is* to lock her in the bathroom. I haven't done it yet. You see, my plan has two parts. The first is to get Boon into the kind of mess she'll have to ask me, and only me, to help her out of. The second is to write a book about it. But I got too excited and started the second part of my plan before I did the first. You don't mind, do you?

Right now, I'm sitting in the bathtub in the bathroom at the Bandellos' house waiting for Boon to come in. There's a blue shower curtain with lily pads on it. And guess what. The Bandellos have one of those sponges that looks like a slice of watermelon. When Boon comes in, I'll jump out of the bathtub, lock the door, and fix the handle so she can't turn it.

I know. I can hear you thinking, What kind of guy is this anyway? I knew he was a lunatic from the very first sentence of this stupid book. Forget it. I'm through!

Please don't stop reading. I'm nervous enough about this plan without having to worry about whether or not you're out there. Stick with me. I'm not as gruesome as I sound. You don't think I'll leave Boon locked in here, do you? I'll let her out when she asks me to help her. And she will. Know why?

Because she won't have anyone else to ask. Have you ever accidentally locked yourself in a bathroom in someone else's house? Or have you ever thought for a moment that you *might* have locked yourself in a bathroom in someone else's house? It's no fun. Especially if the house belongs to the Bandellos. Take my word for it, Boon would rather stay in the bathroom forever than humiliate herself by banging on the door and screaming "Hey, someone! Let me out of here! I'm locked in the bathroom!"

So she'll be stuck. But not really, because I'll be here. And I'll be screaming as loudly as I can, "Boon, this is O'Diddy! Remember? O'Diddy! Boon! Ask me for help! You'll be out of here in no time! Just ask!" And I'll shout that over and over again. And eventually she'll get it as a sort of idea that niggles in the pit of her stomach. And then that stomachy feeling will turn into a voice. My voice. You know what you humans sometimes call "the voice inside"? Well, that's your imaginary friend talking. Or yelling. Some of you listen. Others don't. But Boon will. She's rare and special, even though she's pretending not to be. Besides, she'll have no choice. She'll be locked in the bathroom.

My plan's not really so mean, now, is it?

That's not what Gnomey said. He's like you. He thinks I'm going too far. We were talking about it while Boon was packing for the slumber party.

"What's with you?" he said, after staring at me for ages with his beady little eyes. "I thought you said the house wasn't haunted. Well, if it's not haunted, why do you look so scared?"

"I'm not scared," I said. "I'm thinking."

"'Bout what?" said Gnomey.

I told him it was none of his business, but then he jumped up and down and said I was being stinky, which I was. So, in a weak moment, I told him about my plan. And he told me I was going too far. He even felt sorry for Boon. "Look at her," he said. "She's worried enough without you making it worse."

I watched Boon flutter around the room like a nervous butterfly who thought if she sat down on a flower it might blow up. Boon was choosing everything she needed for the big slumber party and placing each item carefully in a little bag she'd borrowed from her mother.

As she fluttered she muttered, something she always does when she's worried or excited or both. "Oh, what if I get lost in that house? Then Cassie will think I'm stupid and she'll probably never speak to me again." She inspected her nightgown. "Oh, no! It's got raspberry jam on it! What will Mrs. Bandello think?" She spit on a piece of Kleenex and rubbed the spot of jam until it blended in with the flowers on the material. Then she went on to the next worry. "What happens if they have canned peas for dinner?" Boon hates canned peas. Then she stopped fluttering for a second, struck by a thought so horrible she could barely move. "What if . . . what if I throw up?"

For a moment I almost gave up the whole plan. Gnomey was right. Boon was making it bad enough for herself. She didn't need me, her imaginary friend—someone who loves her and is supposed to protect her, not lock her in bathrooms—making it worse. But then Boon's mother said it was time to go, and the next thing I knew we were in the car.

Boon's mother knew Boon was a wreck.

"Boon, there's no point in working yourself up into such a snit. If you keep worrying, you're going to make yourself sick! Now take a deep breath. You'll be fine." Before Boon could say another "Yes, but what if—" we were pulling up outside the Bandellos' house.

Let me tell you right now that if I was the kind of guy who believed in ghosts, this would be the kind of house I'd think they

lived in. It's big and creaky, with lots of dark windows.

As we walked toward the front porch, Boon suddenly stopped. "Mother," she said in a croaky whisper. "I think I've just come down with a terrible case of laryngitis."

"Give me a break," said her mother.

"No, really!" croaked Boon. "Let's go home quick and I'll call Cassie up and tell her. I could be contagious!"

Boon had actually pulled this same stunt to get out of her cousin Herbert's birthday barbecue.

But just then Cassie and Frank threw open the door. "Hi, Boon! Hey, Pickle! Ella! Boon's here!" And you know what? Boon suddenly forgot to be scared. She quickly kissed her mother good-bye, and we went in.

7. Go!

Cassie's friends Pickle and Ella were chasing each other around, giggling up a storm. I could tell it was going to be some party. When we walked in, Ella said, "Let's play hide-and-spook! Boon can be It!"

"Hey, that's not fair!" said Frank. "Boon's never been in this house before!" I told you Frank was nice. And Boon thought so too. I could tell by the way she turned all red.

"Jerkhead's right," said Cassie. "We'll have a tour and play follow the leader at the same time! I'm the leader!"

So we all followed Cassie around the house. While we held our noses and hopped on one foot, we saw Frank's room. Then we walked like elephants into Cassie's room, where we'd be sleeping. We looked at the living room upside down through our legs, and then we crawled into the den. We had to walk backward down the basement stairs. Good thing the attic was off-limits—I was getting exhausted!

After we jumped through the kitchen and did leap twirls into the dining room, Cassie opened the door to Mr. Bandello's workshop.

"We're not allowed in here, but Dad said I could show you the chairs he's making," said Cassie. "Aren't they cool?"

And cool they were. The chairs were for a film called *Torture Chamber*. They were all black, with snakes painted on them. And they had clamps for your arms and clamps for your legs.

"Once you're clamped in, you can't move," said Frank. "Then the real torture begins!" He pulled some fake vampire fangs out of his pocket and put them into his mouth. "Mwha, ha, ha, ha, ha, ha!" he yelled. That was enough to send everyone screaming out of the room—including me.

To finish the tour Cassie showed us a few closets and then the little room where Mrs. Bandello practiced her cello. I still hadn't seen one bathroom.

There's got to be a bathroom! I was thinking. You can't have a house without a bathroom, can you? No sooner had the thought filled my head when Cassie said, "Oh, yes, and here's the bathroom."

And I've been in here ever since.

As I write this, everyone's still playing hide-and-spook. What happens is, one person's It. You turn out the lights and It counts to one hundred. Meanwhile, everyone else hides. Then It goes around looking for everyone in the dark. The people who are hiding have to make some kind of spooky noise to give It a clue. If It gets close enough, whoever's hiding jumps out and scares It.

But if It can manage to sneak up on whoever's hiding without the hider knowing, It scares that person. Get it? Scare or be scared. I know it sounds stupid. But you might not think so if you could see this house. You know I don't go in for ghosts and things, but I tell you, it's spooky here in the dark.

Uh-oh. I just heard Boon say "Where's the bathroom again?" Here she comes! This is the moment I've been waiting for! Wish me luck. I'll let you know what happens as soon as I can.

8. Oops!

You aren't going to believe what just happened to me.

I was so sure it was Boon that I just reached out from behind the shower curtain and locked the door and fixed the handle. Then I heard someone whisper, "Now where did Mom put the washcloths? I can't drop a wet washcloth on somebody without a washcloth, can I?" That someone wasn't Boon. It was Cassie.

For the first time in my life I was glad I'm invisible.

Cassie finally found a washcloth and soaked it in cold water. Then she went to leave, but she couldn't get out. I wonder why. So you know what she did? She banged on the door and yelled, "Hey, somebody! I'm locked in the bathroom! Let me out!"

Her father had to take the door handle off with a screwdriver. And then he said, "Why do you kids lock these doors? You know the locks in this house are weird."

"But I didn't lock the door, Dad! Promise!" said Cassie.

Her father studied the lock. "Well, I wouldn't be surprised if these things locked by themselves. They're ancient. Listen, if anyone else gets stuck, just bang on the door. I'll save you!" Then he went off mumbling, "When this *Torture Chamber* job is over, I'm going to use the money to buy new locks for the whole house."

"Your dad's nice," Pickle said.

"I'm glad it wasn't me locked in that bathroom!" said Boon.

"Yeah," said Frank. "I could've been hiding . . . in the toilet!" And then he put in his fangs again and made a noise that sounded like a cross between the Dispatcher blowing her nose and a sick walrus. Everyone ran

squealing and laughing out of the room. Except me.

I guess there's really no point in going on.

My plan failed, and that's that. Listen. I really wouldn't blame you now if you gave this book away. I hope you didn't get peanut butter on it or anything. If you did, ask your imaginary friend to help you get it off. Even if you don't think you've ever had an imaginary friend, just say, "Imaginary friend, whoever you are, help me get the peanut butter off this book so I can give it to my worst enemy." And then see what happens. You might be surprised. And then do me a favor. No, I'm not going to ask you to change your mind and keep the book. I'm going to ask you to be a rare and special human. I'm going to ask you to keep asking your imaginary friend for help. Then your imaginary friend won't feel invisible anymore. Like I do.

Oh, the misery!

I hate giving up, but I know when I'm beat. It's been nice knowing you. Wait a minute—I don't know you. Okay, so it's been nice having you know me. I'm going to get out of the bathtub now. Bye.

THE END

Hold it! Wait a minute! Stop! Thank goodness you're still here! Guess what! Something's happened! Something wonderful and fantastic! I'm so excited I can barely write! But I'll try.

Right after Cassie got "mysteriously" locked in the bathroom, they all decided to play one more game of hide-and-spook. And Boon was It. Having nothing better to do, since I'd finished my book and said good-bye to you, I decided to follow her around while she looked for everybody.

Boon counted to one hundred and then set out to look for her friends. Every now and then she stopped to listen. Was that *shhhhhhshhhh* noise coming from behind the sofa? Or what about the *fffffffwittt*? Was it someone hiding under the stairs? But then there was a very distinct *plernk* which came from Mr. Bandello's workshop. Boon tiptoed to the doorway. I could've told her there was no one in there, but why waste my breath? She wouldn't hear me anyway.

"Well, it won't hurt if I just have a look . . . " she said, and crept in. I followed and, without thinking, closed the door. *Click.* I've got to tell you, once the door was closed, this room was dark. Boon hates the dark, so she ran toward the door to get out. And you know what happened? She tripped and landed right in one of the chairs!

Clamp! Clunk!

"Oh, no!" she whispered. *"Oh, no!"*

Boon was stuck, and how.

I suddenly saw an opportunity so huge it practically knocked me off my imaginary feet.

Fact one: Boon was not allowed in the room where she was now sitting. Fact two: Boon was not only sitting in the room, she was clamped down. Fact three: Because she wasn't allowed in this room, she couldn't ask anyone to get her out. Fact four: She'd have to ask me.

So what did I do? Exactly what any self-respecting, desperate imaginary friend would do. I started screaming as loudly as I could, "Boon, it's O'Diddy! Boon! I'll help you! Just ask!"

As usual, Boon didn't hear me. She just kept whimpering, "Oh, no! Oh, no! Oh, no! Oh, no!"

"Boon! It's O'Diddy!" I yelled. "I'm here!

Just say 'O'Diddy, help me get out of this!' and I will! You don't even have to say 'Please'!"

Then she said, "If I call for help, they'll find me in here. Mr. Bandello will be so angry. They'll send me home for sure. Then Cassie and Frank will never speak to me again. And they'll tell everyone at school. I'll never be invited to a slumber party ever again. Ever!"

She was getting frantic, so I kept yelling. "Boon! Just ask O'Diddy! Do you hear me? O'Diddy!"

"But if I stay here for too long, they'll come looking for me. And then they'll find me! That's even worse! Oh, what am I going to do?"

She grunted and groaned and tried to get out, but it was no use. If you ever see *Torture Chamber,* I want to tell you right now that the chairs really work.

Boon kept struggling and I kept screaming, but it wasn't doing either of us any good. "Boon!" I hollered. I was getting hoarse. "This is your last chance! I know you don't want to hear me, but I'm going to tell you one last time. O'Diddy's here! I want to help!

Please! Ask me! Ask O'Diddy! DO YOU HEAR ME?—O'DIDDY!"

All of a sudden she stopped squirming. "Huh?" she said. At first I didn't know whether it was a grunt or a question, but it was the first sign of hope I'd had in years. So I kept yelling.

"O'Diddy! O'Diddy! I'm here! I'll help! Ask me and you'll be out of here in a minute!"

"O'Diddy?" she said. "Why am I thinking about O'Diddy? I haven't thought about him in ages."

Too true.

Then she started to cry. It almost broke my heart. "Oh, what am I going to do? Here I am clamped in one of Mr. Bandello's special chairs and I'm thinking about O'Diddy. Oh, O'Diddy, I miss you now. If only I were three and you were here to help me!"

"I am!" I screamed. "Ask me! Oh, Boon! Please ask me to help!"

Suddenly she stopped crying. "O'Diddy?" she whispered, so softly I could barely hear her. "No, this is stupid."

"No, it's not!" I yelled it right into her ear.

"Oh, who cares if it's stupid?" she said.

"Atta girl! Oh, ask me! Ask me! Ask me!"

Boon took a deep breath. "O'Diddy, if you're here, could you help me? Please? I need you. Help me get out of here!"

How many times I'd wanted to hear her say those words!

I leaped into action. I pushed one set of clamps as hard as I could with my feet and pulled the other as hard as I could with my hands. Boon tried to stand up again. Thanks to me, the clamps came undone! Boon was free!

She ran to the door. Then she stopped. "O'Diddy, if that really was you, I promise I'll never forget you again. Never."

9. The End for Real This Time

She won't forget me, you know. Because she's rare and special, after all. I knew it all the time.

Boon doesn't actually see me with her eyes, but she knows what I feel like—a birthday party, remember? And as long as she can feel me, she'll know I'm there. And as long as she knows I'm there, I'm not invisible.

And boy, does it feel good.

Before I write THE END for real, I want to thank you for sticking with me all the way through this book. It wasn't so bad, was it?

I don't know what you look like, but if you ever meet a girl named Boon, try to slip the name O'Diddy into the conversation. If the

Boon you're with is my Boon — and I ask you, how many Boons can there be, anyway? — then I'll be there and I'll know you're you. And if your imaginary friend doesn't mind, I'll give you a big kiss right on your nose. To say thank you. So if you meet my Boon and you say something like, "Say, don't you have a cousin or something called O'Diddy?" and then your nose itches, you'll know why.

Until then, bye!

THE END

About the Author

JOCELYN STEVENSON has written magazine articles, books, and television programs for children. She says that she got the idea for *O'Diddy* about ten years ago and has been thinking about it on and off ever since. Finally she wrote it down. "I didn't know about imaginary friends when I was little," she says, "but I know about them now. It's never too late, and you're never too old, to have one."

She lives with her husband, three young children, and their dogs Cassie and Frankie about fifteen miles outside Edinburgh.

About the Illustrator

SUE TRUESDELL is a well-known children's book illustrator. She didn't have an *invisible* friend when she was little, but she says, "I used to talk to my shadow—that was my imaginary friend." Sue Truesdell has illustrated many books for young readers, including *Lily and the Runaway Baby, Addie Meets Max, Addie Runs Away, Donna O'Neeshuck Was Chased by Some Cows,* and *The Golly Sisters Go West.*